PRAISE FOR GORMAN POETRY

"Slightly lilting verse guides like a fast-moving laser through widely different topics, anchoring them with subtle verbal acrobatics into a pleasant and cohesive unit. *Poems of Life, Love, and the Meaning of Meaning* is a volume of self-help advice in a poetic format, a unique concept that delighted me... with a dry and witty take on life that flashed out like lightning... A highly individual book that will be enjoyed by minds that like to roam the galaxy in brief poetic installments."

—Sarah Scheele, *Readers' Favorite*

"A reflective experience that is both gentle in touch and penetrating in depth... The collection reminds me of the luminosity of a watercolor painting where bits of the underlayment shine through... Deceptively simple, the images the poems produce are thought-provoking without being heavy-handed or moralizing... The light-hearted approach to serious matters will appeal to many readers and makes this collection a perfect gift for friends and family who may just need a little prod toward healing and love."

—Kimberlee J. Benart, *Readers' Favorite*

OTHER WORKS BY THIS AUTHOR

*Poems of Life, Love
and the Meaning of Meaning*

Sojourn

The Lightness of Being

Infinite Healing Trilogy:

Poems and Messages for the Loss of a Loved One

*Poems and Messages for the Loss of Your
Animal Companion*

Healed in Timelessness

POET GONE WILD

More Matters of Love and Death

Gorman Poetry

Copyright © 2020, 2024 Paul J. Gorman
All Rights Reserved

Year of the Book
135 Glen Avenue
Glen Rock, PA 17327

ISBN: 978-1-64649-412-5 (paperback)
ISBN: 978-1-64649-413-2 (ebook)

No part of this publication may be reproduced, distributed, or transmitted in any form or by any means, including photocopying, recording, or other electronic or mechanical methods, without the prior written permission of the author, except in the case of brief quotations embodied in critical reviews and certain other noncommercial uses permitted by copyright law.

DISCLAIMER: The poems in this book are solely the opinions of the author, fully intended to diagnose, prevent, and heal ailments of the body and mind through the spirit. Seek medical attention when necessary.

TABLE OF CONTENTS

*When life in motion needs meaning,
find it in emotion —
love, wonder, quiet reflection, and joy.*

—*Spirit message*

THAT WAS MY DREAM

That was my dream
on which my heart was set
but like most dreams
I was designed to forget

though my heart doesn't know
or it's trying to get
the millions of pieces
that were part of that set

NOTHING I KNOW

I told her I couldn't
  (long ago)
live without her
    and now I don't know

if nothing meant 'no'
    and I should go
a life unspent
    is nothing I know

nothing I eat
    and nothing I sleep
nothing I think
    and nothing I keep

will help me forget
    or let me forego
my life without her
    is nothing, I know

MY HARDEST TASK

How can I not
 live in the past
when you were my future
 now here at last

here alone
 tied to the mast
sirens of memories
 our times that have passed

I played my part
 but was poorly cast
now looking back
 I should have asked

how can I not
 live in the past
when you were my future
 my hardest task

NOTE TO SELF

<do not reply>

I think my issue
   that's denied and delayed
and needs to heal
   is having been betrayed

not just by others
   that were on my side
or by myself
   if I look inside

did I try
   her eyes didn't lie
I won't know why
   but need to decide

am I betrayed by life
   my trusted guide
I know how it plans
   to slip off and die

<do not reply>

A COLLEGE PRANK
ON ST. JOHN'S LAWN

I thought it would be funny
  enlisting others in my scheme
to point up at the sky
    amazed by what we had seen

there it is again
    others came running around
they saw it too
    unsure of what we had found

an alien craft
    now out of sight and sound
had they looked down
    they'd have seen a clown on the ground

(the aliens were clever
    not letting them see
what was in front of them
    now forever affecting me)

*but some did witness the invisible scene

FOR OUR LOVE TO GROW

Something I noticed
　　long ago
is that the best people
　　are often the first to go

do they know something
　　that we don't know
the ultimate secret
　　and not let it show

except for their gifts
　　that life bestows
accepted by us
　　for our love to grow

A THOUSAND DEATHS

I'd rather die
    a thousand deaths
than to hurt her
    so now I guess

I'll die again
    then more for sure
and now I know
    what reincarnation's for

NOW AND TOGETHER

Now you know
   I'm a tortured soul
self-defeat
   taking its toll

I cannot forget
   the time we met
or get beyond
   my deepest regret

and blame myself
   that we're apart
taking the blame
   we did not start

there's no one else
   that I can name
to share the guilt
   regret and shame

so I'll hang on
   and not forgive instead
until the end
   and my blame is dead

Let me help you
*   and make this clear*
if you had gone there
*   you would not be here*

talk about failure
*   and a life of regret*
Door Number One
*   was your less optimal bet*

unlimited realities
*   and probabilities to know*
each one valid
*   created all in a row*

on a line in time
*   only forward to go*
reflecting on choices
*   so awareness can grow*

but try to focus
*   or at least to allow*
the present moment
*   that is here and how*

you continue creating
*   your universe with me*
love it, we'll live it
*   now and together, you'll see*

ACCEPTANCE AND PEACE

Time can fly
 and keeps marching on
but not my doubts
 that should be gone

they stay with my fears
 old regrets and pains
living for years
 they always remain

why don't they die
 what do they want
self-love and forgiveness
 until we are the same

one body, one mind
 judgments released
one love, one healing
 in acceptance and peace

MY FUTURE SELF

My future self
is only doing
what I'm doing now
    and can show me how

there's no need to fear
    what I see or hear
it had once been me
    right here, this year

it had also wondered
    what I would become
as a future self
    in our future as one

that has healed old pains
    more losses than gains
and still have joyful
    memories remain

that is my wish
    for my future self
joyful presence remains
    in the present I became

MY LUCK HAD RUN OUT

I was afraid of my fear
   not sure of my doubt
robbed by a need
   lack endured without

my confidence that sank
   when hope disappeared
trust went away
   love used to be near

my luck had run out
   but I never knew
that it was about to come back
   and bring back you

ALL I WANT

All I want
    is a peaceful life
some meaningful work
    and a friend in my wife

I'd be pleased
    to have two of these
but won't have peace
    without number 3

so how could she
    be a friend to me
unless I am the friend
    she needs me to be

A SIGN

Today I saw
    a cancer center
it was called 'Progressive'
    but who would enter

for a conventional answer
    with a name like this
'Progressive Cancer'
    well I guess it fits

Enter at
    your own risk

how about a sign
    that's much more benign
'Wellness Aligned'
    should be the line

but they'd have to support
     your body's design
not start a war
     and you'd be fine

restoring the body
     and easing the mind
with what they need
     and they would find

It heals itself
     in progressive time

LOVE ALWAYS SHOWS

What is love
    a word used a lot
and whatever it is
    I know what it's not

maybe it's kindness
    patience and peace
stillness in motion
    or a feeling released

of peace flowing out
    that allows flowing in
a two-way street
    beginning within

either way makes both
    and requires a flow
by loving yourself
    is where it starts and goes

a feedback loop
    God only knows
from inside of you
    love always shows

??

I am just
   a human being
and a human doing
   feeling and seeing

a small collection
   of contradictions agreeing
to disagree
   which should be freeing

always changing
   as perceived by me
life arranging
   as I believe it to be

in a cooperative world
   from the trees to the sea
any disagreement
   is inside of me

IT FEELS LIKE ME

A little richer
　a little stronger
a little kinder
　　and patient longer

that's what I see
　　as my immediate needs
so how would it feel
　　having all of these

it feels more free
　　and the way to be
making it real
　　it feels like me

SUPPORT YOUR LOCAL
OR NON-LOCAL HEALER

What a healer discerned
   and I had learned
is that feelings sent out
   are then returned

as emotions turned in
   from where they begin
projecting out
   but always within

so how do I feel
   either well or not
however I felt
   is how that I got

a pain inside
   from the feelings denied
run more tests
   is how doctors decide

if they only knew
        what makes ailments real
feelings coming through
        for me to heal

so I ask myself
        if my body lies
or is there something else
        I try to hide

CUSTOMER SERVICE

The checkout clerk
  had asked if I got
all I was looking for
  and I said I had not

do you sell a strawberry
  heart repair
sweet peace in a can
  or a smile I can wear

and corrective glasses
  to make memories fair
and heal old wounds
  I need a pair

I could have gone on
  but saw in his stare
I was not ready for checkout
  and he pointed to where

I saw Customer Service
  and God was there
ready to help me
  and make me aware

Feel free to sit down
    there appeared a chair
life is change
    which can create despair

it's easy to think
    that I don't care
and life is hard
    or it isn't fair

but change is good
    always in the air
to create what you want
    and make more to share

I am all and you
    so we won't compare
choosing love in each moment
    will be our prayer

So how could it be
    that God would appear
at Customer Service
    Employee of the Year?

You had asked for help
    I heard in my ear
when choosing love
    it brings you near

love is sincere
        God without fear
fear interferes
        now it is clear

Then let me ask you
        while I am here
what am I afraid of
        even afraid to hear?

That you could fail
        will be alone
or judged by others
        with nothing to own

it either isn't possible
        or is not true
doesn't matter
        or is not for you

when you choose love
        in whatever you do
loving life and yourself
        you choose me too

WE CAN BE

I had confided
    in God last night
that I don't know Godness
    except in what's right

and even so
    it's subject to change
just a matter of opinion
    in our domain

based on perception
    through our beliefs
the Godness inception
    created in peace

or in a big bang
    a violent release
an immaculate conception
    the wonders won't cease

so let me know
    and let it rhyme
please tell me the story
    the beginning of time

I wanted to see
what you would do
given a surprise
the mystery of you

would you love it
or send it back
not even see it
or need to attack

your own creation
not subject to lack
your mental projection
as a matter of fact

that was the best
that I could give
your freedom to act
and a will to live

Thanks so much!
a universal gift
one size fits all
I love what you did

or was it done by me
a projection to see
and to know the Godness
that we can be

SOMEONE LIKE ME

The hardest poem
  I ever had to write
is what do I like
    most about life

it has to be real
    and help me to deal
with healing myself
    and the way that I feel

I could drink a bottle
    of mental floss
pick up the pieces
    or put off the cost

heads you win
    tails I lost
is life the coin
    or a coin toss

I'm tired of grieving
    leaving is believing
how can life be
    healing or relieving

the bravest people
    have long since died
off into something
    I'm not willing to try

rolling through space
    making good time
never in one place
    our planet's design

always in motion
    leaving the past behind
wisdom surpassing
    our hearts and minds

what is oneness
    unless one means mine
and God is Godness
    with no timeline

that's all fine
    I can always decline
what do I like
    what can I find

I love to see goodness
    and I try to be kind
and help other beings
    that are left in a bind

no need to remind
    that I'd cry when I see
one day stars had aligned
    and I need someone like me

YOU'LL KNOW WHAT IS REAL

I get a high score
    for being ignored
ninety percent
    or even more

no hello or thank you
    no email reply
they all went to lunch
    and walked on by

I see the cameras
    wherever I go
do they see me
    what fear do they know

I suppose that I
    could be a ghost
an earthbound spirit
    without a host

that's the problem
    to know where I stand
but not understanding
    where I am

caught in a time
    on an intangible line
to always keep up
    or be left behind

out in the cosmos
    I'd never survive
out of my mind
    I am still alive

10 million miles
    in outer space
there is no earth
    no time, no place

at the speed of light
    a blistering pace
it would take all day
    to rejoin the race

but past a point
    too far, too fast
time has stopped
    no future, no past

if I could go back
    would I expect to see
one thousand years
    had healed humanity

or did they die off
    long before
selfish choices
    they could not afford

what I hope to see
    and the cameras record
is that fear was ignored
    and respect restored

what do you think
    a simple wish
respectfulness
    with fears dismissed

Life comes from your mind
    with thoughts that are kind
or if they are not
    I think you will find

they come from a fear
    and lies held dear
that you are separate
    and don't want to hear

unless it is love
    because that's what you are
both here and now
    neither near nor far

If I am love
    then how could it be
that fear and judgment
    could come from me?

*That is your choice
    your will is free
imagine a world
    where you'll never see*

*fear or mistrust
    and lack goes bust
only illusions
    and illusions are just*

*imagined by you
    creative tools
to find your way
    on a ship of fools*

*not a judgment
    just stating your case
you also created
    the time and place*

*you are love
    and love is all
so you are me
    and you would recall*

until you forgot
    and dreamed you were not
wake up dreamer
    you imagined a lot

If people are love
    then how can they hate
why can't they see
    what they create?

That was another
    aspect you chose
in a dream of yourself
    so love always shows

Thank you for that
    and now that I know
I am you and love
    with fears to let go

is it possible
    to be awake in a dream
where nothing is real
    despite what it seems?

Yes, it is so
    and now you will see
that one thing is real
    your love is me

and we are one
*   so go back to your wish*
and love yourself
*   since only one exists*

Thank you again
    I won't choose to ignore
unless it's a fear
    and I'll see what it's for

Life is to heal
*   and when you can feel*
that your love is me
*   you'll know what is real*

ONLY MYSELF

You know what's true
love creates love
peace creates peace
and it comes to you

or more precisely
it also comes through
it's what you want
and what you do

Then why do I live
on a planet of egos
I hope we're not one
or not more than two

Yes, you're correct
whatever you project
will always connect
the cause and effect

you are the cause
first and without flaws
the dream and the dreamer
of immutable laws

bent or broken
*   no punishment or fine*
there's only one law
*   and it's really not mine*

do as you please
*   you are free to be*
and punish yourself
*   until you can see*

love creates love
*   peace creates peace*
coming through you
*   which brings you to me*

who am I ?
*   I thought you'd never ask*
how should I put this
*   I'm like light through a glass*

frequency and light
*   and vibrations you receive*
actually don't exist
*   without you to perceive*

as they come through
*   what you believe*
and how you feel
*   is where you conceive*

that is our oneness
     I am light in your mind
photons of healing
     for our love to shine

What creates light
     and where do I find
the source of the oneness
     making our space and time?

You create it yourself
     and the kaleidoscope you see
that's the one law
     the way you want it to be

which needs an ego
     to not be dismissed
each unique awareness
     that spirit enlists

Then why should I care
     or need to be aware
especially on a planet
     where life isn't fair?

That would be fine
     if that's what you choose
whatever it is
     it's coming from you

some blame me
*   which brings us back*
to our photons of light
*   with an absence of lack*

you create all moments
*   back to back*
our peace and love
*   and whatever you attract*

when you set fear free
*   you and I then agree*
peace and love can shine
*   clear from eternity*

beyond the glass
*   only oneness can be*
projecting our healing
*   where you and I become we*

what irritation
*   was on your mind*
and needed to define
*   egos as unaligned?*

we had agreed
*   to disagree*
that you'd be apart
*   but free to be*

life healing itself
of the guilt it seems
believing that oneness
is an impossible dream

that is the place
where your ego begins
in your own creation
that you created within

separate from oneness
if there is such a thing
the big illusion
only a projection can bring

creating a world
that illuminates all else
finding oneness aware of
only myself

THERE'S ALWAYS HOPE

Who are you
    I wish I knew
and would like to hear it
    in a verse or two

I am light
    and the frequencies beyond
illuminating your now
    for you to respond

delighted as life
    life heals itself
I am the light
    in each of your cells

that's what I am
    bright from your core
an aura enlightened
    and Godness of yours

that's really it
    and you are free to choose
there is no winner
    when you cannot lose

what I suggest
    is to do your best
it's your adventure
    and is not a test

inside is out
    with outside in
and here is where
    your dream begins

infinite life
    either way
into the light
    when you pass away

and back to me
    where you always were
unlimited love
    you are always pure

as you read this
    and know for sure
I am the light of the world
    that will heal and cure

healing yourself
    with feelings you use
there's always hope
    that it's me you choose

A PERFECT FIT

What are they thinking
    dressed in white and black
ambassadors of faith
    that keep coming back

"The Book is true
    and He is good.
Prepare for God
    the way we should."

Am I to assume
    that He's a male too
ready to judge
    and working with you?

and if He is
    would He be fair
why would He care
    what does He wear?

I'll ask Him myself
	bring the truth to bare
I need a few answers
	if He would so dare

I am a woman
	not to compare
and also a man
	for a human pair

I am a tree
	the sea and a bear
a mountain peak
	and a solar flare

I am light
	and I am the air
to answer your question
	what do I wear

I am you
	so you are where
we are love
	and as love we share

to send and receive
no need to believe
since I am you
I cannot leave

whatever you choose
lose or refuse
I am with you
as the love we use

I am also them
not easily deceived
except in the idea
that I need to be pleased

they're happy to share
and want you to heal
gaining new wisdom
that spirit reveals

maybe they came
because they knew
or looking for Godness
drew them to you

bless them, bless me
and you will see
the loving spirit
we can freely be

peace and compassion
are what we wear
always in fashion
and dressed with flair

love is Godness
received and deserved
weaving creation
with your thoughts and words

so think of me
and how we can be
a perfect fit
clothed in humanity

(I am one with you
as a singular me
rather than He or She
let's say 'We')

YOU'LL LOVE WHEN YOU SEE

The universe responds
    to nothing else
but the way I feel
    about myself

do I feel neglected
    affected and rejected
or do I feel loved
    accepted and protected

and not just loved
    in a receiving role
but being the love
    and I am the Whole

pretty amazing
    that the universe could be
an extension of feelings
    only coming from me

so I flow the source
      through a prism of feelings
my life creation
      made real for self-healing

let's go inside
      to examine this
where there's only peace
      and all time exists

what does it prove
      what does it need
infinite energy
      to be coming through me?

*It wants to feel
      and it wants to do
its own magnificence
      as me and you*

Does it really need me
      can't it just be
does it need mixed feelings
      that don't agree?

maybe that's it
    and what it asks of me
is to love myself
    and love I will see

a little tricky
    now I feel apart
let's try again
    and each moment I start

I am compassion
    so will not get mad
I have no fear
    but can still be sad

I am complete
    love comes from within
all time and creation
    about to begin

does that make sense
    that life starts here
there is no offense
    to create anger or fear?

then you haven't seen
    my daily commute
reckless drivers that speed
    all along my route

you should see at work
    the laziness and greed
and on the computer
    deception and need

or in the news
    playing violent feeds
our Garden of Eden
    growing lots of weeds

This week it will change
    when you stand in your power
you'll love when you see
    each weed is a flower

ONE AND A PAIR

What would you see
if you were in my shoes?
That you are me
and cannot lose

you are free to be
whatever you choose
no need to agree
with others' views

they provide a contrast
for you to use
red or blue
in a million hues

I wish you were here
to sit with me
just to talk
and to have some tea

That doesn't work
for us to be two
as I was saying
I am you

back to the colors
*   and what I would see*
your beautiful painting
*   creating a world with me*

I guess that explains
    why no one paints you
they paint everything else
    to mixed reviews

It doesn't matter
*   and I am there*
as you the viewer
*   and what the painter prepares*

for better or worse
*   through wear and tear*
it's our creation
*   you're encouraged to share*

when you follow your passion
*   you're alive and aware*
both subject and object
*   coming together to where*

we are both one
*   inspired to care*
and in your shoes
*   we are one and a pair*

WHICH IS WHICH

Some people think
    that I don't exist
that they are real
    and on this they insist

perhaps I do
    and here's a twist
maybe they don't
    so consider this

that they could be
    in my imagination
the missing link
    in my miscreation

aware of itself
    and wondering why
what went wrong
    and who am I

which brings us back
*   to which one is real*
who's certain to die
*   and hurting to heal*

deal me in
*   on the karmic wheel*
you're how I love
*   and how I feel*

it's kind of surreal
*   for us to switch*
to heal through you
*   now which is which*

feeling through you
*   now healing through me*
which is which
*   which will we be*

AS GOOD AS IT GETS

Only thirty
or forty more years
life measured in time
in laughter and tears

what did I gain
what did I fear
what does it matter
why am I here

I can't say that I know
or at least it's not clear
but if I had to guess
why I chose to appear

it would be to express
life now at its best
its creative awareness
and I'm here as a guest

both student and teacher
    taking the same test
I'm not finished yet
    how much time is left

what if I fail
    only seeing the worst
I could be the last
    but won't be the first

I'll take my time
    and will do my best
to try seeing life
    as good as it gets

(the time could be less)

LIFE IS ALWAYS TODAY

Do you expect
   me to believe
I was born only once
   and then I will leave

wouldn't it make sense
   if I could incarnate then
it would be just as easy
   to do it again

or more than once
   all at the same time
many appearances
   and each one mine?

Yes, it's true
   each life is new
and never through
   you just choose a new view

for what you will do
    in conditions you create
as yourself
    you may love to hate

or hate to love
    either way
love is there
    and there to stay

for you to allow
    a Groundhog Day to replay
only for love
    life is always today

MEANING THAT LIVES

What's the point
    of being alive
what's the purpose
    why even try

where's the meaning
    in trying to survive
knowing I'm leaving
    but not why I arrived

You came to be
    and you came to do
free to see
    what you can improve

or to destroy
    and create anew
or not see at all
    if you so choose

it happens a lot
  you'll see in the news
how people forgot
  or simply refuse

to honor life
  and each other's views
or respect themselves
  by speaking the truth

so consider this
  that the meaning is
by loving yourself
  you're loving what is

to heal in time
  love receives and gives
you are my divine
  meaning that lives

STILL WITH ME

*What did you think
of your time on earth
what does it mean
    what was it worth?*

*do you want to go back
    and live it again
it's easily arranged
    just say when*

*how did it feel
    I know it seemed real
how did you manage
    did you manage to heal?*

*as creation released
    from your thoughts and beliefs
with everyday miracles
    created in peace*

I was there
    your stillness within
and always with you
    where we would begin

right or wrong
    blessing or sin
we'll try again
    you can only win

because you are free
    to see how to be
still within
    you are still with me

EACH DREAM HAS A HALF-LIFE

The day will come
 when I am done
my days all numbered
 starting with one

how many more
 another has begun
as many as I need
 so let it be fun

each day has a half-life
 of ten to twelve hours
to make magical moments
 with our magical powers

of kindness and love
 and a generous spirit
I didn't forget
 but still need to hear it

live your dream
 don't delay one minute
each dream has a half-life
 but is whole with you in it

(living it and loving it)

YOUR POINT WITHIN
(A POINT HAS NO DIMENSION)

Who is God
  please tell me again
start at the beginning
  beginning with when

I am the light
  and you are the lens
and we are both
  it all depends

on which end receives
  and which end sends
unless in a circle
  that continuously bends

picture a point
  the center of a sphere
call it Godness
  and you are here

a point in your mind
    just to be clear
your life as a center
    in a God atmosphere

now turned inside out
    the sphere is within
the entire cosmos
    on the head of a pin

all in a photon
    no size, no mass
either particle or wave
    no time to pass

all from a point
    infinite space and time
where All is one
    a still point in your mind

what that means
    is that I am you
there is no without
    except in your view

looking out
*   to infinity*
you are Point A
*   and where is Point B?*

it circles back
*   through you to me*
a feedback loop
*   making reality*

to answer your question
*   about where God begins*
in stillness and peace
*   from your point within*

POINT OF VIEW / POINT OF YOU

Why do I have
only spiritual questions
I'd like some answers
or at least some suggestions

You're already aware
that everything spins
so there must be a center
where the motion begins

but the center is still
in a void that you fill
our centered oneness
my point if you will

motion needs time
and movement needs space
going in circles
making a case

that there is a purpose
or a meaning behind
your point in a void
our Godness of mind

What could it be
    that I need to see
as the point of Godness
    from a point in me

raising vibration
    to our point divine
each incarnation
    created in time

a time in space
    where both intersect
which form a grid
    of which I suspect

is spinning too
    and always moves
as we select
    how we flow through

each time and place
    an ever changing view
The point of Godness
    is the point of you

WHAT WOULD A PERFECT WORLD LOOK LIKE?

No animals are harmed
  food's organically farmed
people are peaceful
  no need to be armed

commerce is fair
  talents are shared
water is clean
  as well as the air

only the wisest
  are leaders and teachers
each voice is heard
  and the best are featured

jails are for learning
  working and earning
society's respect
  before returning

drugs are for healing
    and are almost free
what are you smoking
    you might say to me

yes, it's a dream
    and it's almost here
it just needs peace
    love conquers fear

love of life
    to yourself be kind
by loving yourself
    you will find

love in your world
    peace in our time
the peace in our world
    begins in my mind

N.D.E.

Am I in spirit
   or in total denial
no body, no place
   no time, and no trials

funny to see
   looking down at me
what was I doing
   or supposed to be

an achiever, believer
   giver and receiver
now just a body
   with a near-fatal fever

where is my pride
   no place to hide
arrange for a service
   I will need a ride

I am feeling free
    and while alive I tried
to feel this way
    but always denied

loving myself
    and life as my guide
no more to prove
    nothing to decide

oneness in spirit
    no longer an I
only love and awareness
    I finally arrived

AS LONG AS I CHOSE

What if I lived
   as long as I chose
the death of death
   its own death it knows

would I choose forever
   live a continuous run
or decide I'm done
   in century one

then why would I leave
   bring my time to a close
unless I'd had enough
   or was overexposed

to one-way streets
   and egos that know
couldn't find my peace
   or I felt transposed

in mind and body
   with spirit that flows
love and awareness
   fulfills me to go

(back to the love I know)

WE ARE THERE

I caught a glimpse
   and was totally aware
of what heaven is like
   and we are there

an afternoon party
   a family affair
surrounded by love
   and without a care

only to share
   life and love as a pair
heaven and earth
   you and I are where

both sides meet
   where here is there
love and life are forever
   we're there now, I swear

NOW AND THEN

Life has limits
	and has to end
it doesn't last
	just where and when

a temporary time
	in a physical place
with everyone else
	deep in outer space

what if there was
	no death or escape
your life was forever
	a long human race

you couldn't die
	but could only try
to find peace of mind
	in all that time

and see the cycles
        of life renew
the death and birth
        of all but you

it makes more sense
        to start again
in different lifetimes
        now and then

THERE IS ONLY LOVE

Now is the time
    to say goodbye
so long, farewell
    I had to die

with no escape
    from ways to try
prisoner of mind
    now free to fly

what can I say
    now that I'm gone
we'll meet again
    before too long

maybe then
    I will know how to act
and not be fooled
    or the fool, in fact

I'll keep my wisdom
    and lessons I've learned
the truth and talents
    that I found and earned

is there more to life
    or was that enough
what I know now
    is that there is only love

AWARENESS MESSAGE

Are we consciously aware after we die?

Not only aware, totally in healed peace and Oneness.

What is that like?

Humans heal illuminated in light, meaning in Godness—only generally healed to mentally learn how life took them to hell or healing heaven that they believe they deserve.

What do we deserve?

Knowing love.

Starting with self-love?

Healing in each moment, allowing love motion.

I understand that the spirit world has vibration, and our physical world has motion—which requires time and space. Please tell me more.

Time motions life, nothing stops. Nothing means half of life in physical reality, all in healed total reality. Nothing means Oneness—no thing, only love.

When we die, our time has stopped, so we cannot have motion and no longer need space—then we exit twoness, returning to Oneness?

Not returning, mind opening into Oneness. Life means half Oneness, and half twoness— Oneness in nothing, and twoness in everything.

I think I know what you are saying—that we are in a total Oneness reality of no motion, conscious of a seemingly separate physical reality in motion?

Motioning only towards love.

So by definition, twoness has to be a part of Oneness—or it wouldn't be Oneness.

Dealing in all time and all things.

And separation is an illusion.

Allowing motion, healing in Godness.

ONE WITH ME

What can I say
   to those bereaved
     their loved ones departed
   absent without leave?

What I can tell you
   is that they are relieved
at Oneness and peace
   in varying degrees

it all depends
   on what they need
who they meet
   and what they believe

One moment of truth
   that we all had agreed
you'd be back home
   to finally breathe

free of disease
   and no longer deceived
eyes now closed
   they can easily see

and also feel
   more than just free
in the Heart of Godness
   they are One with me

What do you mean
   who they meet
is that a first stage
   and then they proceed?

Being conscious
   means to be aware
of something else
   separation's still there

you will meet your loved ones
   who had gone before
to make you feel welcome
   before you learn more

then comes a point
   that's hard to describe
only Oneness of God
   separation has died

no space or time
*   you are all you can be*
love no longer denied
*   when you are One with me*

(the best thing to say
*   to those who stay*
is that you don't really leave
*   it just seems that way*

but they feel grief
*   and need a relief*
time to heal
*   and to feel my peace*

you'll be in a reunion
*   and they'll greet you one day*
the loved ones you miss
*   One with me today)*

Note that our connection to Oneness is love

ON YOUR OWN

The only thing
 I know for sure
is that fear is the problem
 that I need to cure

a fear of lack
 keeps my fears intact
of love and money
 I love in fact

is the purpose of life
 to heal our needs
by how we feel
 then they're real indeed

*Let's look at fear
 now that you asked
not having enough
 or enough to last*

and last until when
*   your very last day*
and who's to say
*   that day's not today*

what will they think
*   you played by the rules*
in a world full of judges
*   that you judged as fools*

I'll tell you a secret
*   that's becoming well known*
that you create your reality
*   so you're on your own*

whatever you see
*   you made it yourself*
so look for solutions
*   you'll see them as well*

on your own
*   means owned by you*
and create means creative
*   it's what you do*

if fear is the problem
*   then what I suggest*
to be truly healed
*   is to put fear to the test*

now imagine yourself
*   on the day you died*
no food or money
*   no silly pride*

it now appears clear
*   with your needs released*
you don't need fear
*   you're in total peace*

on your own
*   and free to be*
no need for needs
*   makes you One with me*

HEART OF GODNESS

I had no self-worth
   right after my birth
not that I can recall
   that or anything at all

no goals or ambition
   no confidence or fear
born in transition
   still in my first year

my greatest achievement
   besides getting here
was being greeted by love
   dear hearts beating near

That's what you know
   because that's what you are
coming from Oneness
   and born with one heart

beating a rhythm
   measures in time
one after the other
   One heartbeat in mine

you came to be
to see what to see
looking for love
because you came from me

you were also taught
that I wouldn't agree
and with that thought
you couldn't be free

Unless I forgive
myself and others
I'd rather not
if I had my druthers

That is fine
but only hurts you
which isn't possible
from our Oneness view

except in your mind
where you crash and burn
and find separation
or refuse to learn

mad at yourself
not allowed to be free
looking around
there is only me

which also includes you
    a Oneness of we
the Heart of Godness
    feeling healed to be

Well, I don't doubt
    that you mean well
with spiritual talk
    in our living hell

what is the point
    of our being here
non-love all around
    in what I see and hear?

Now you have it
    and what I want to make clear
how you feel about yourself
    is where you heal your fear

that is projected out
    finding separate divisions
something to fight
    in your grand Inquisitions

yes, it's hell
    and it won't go away
crashing and burning
    day after day

until you make up your mind
  that the fight is within
conflicted in Oneness
  is as silly as sin

or should I say guilty
  now there's a sore topic
and rightfully so
  until you choose to stop it

which is why you came
  to try again
and enlighten yourself
  to lessen the pain

you think you left Godness
  not possible or true
the physical illusion
  is only coming from you

we're making good progress
  and what I suggest that you do
is to forgive yourself
  for believing it's true

in your own creation
  each moment is new
hearts beating our Oneness
  Heart of Godness is in you

IN YOUR RIGHT MIND

How is Godness
   on this beautiful morning
a funny question
   but worth exploring

to be total Oneness
   love and bliss
wholeness in energy
   of All That Is

as I live within limits
   determined by me
a boundary being
   that will briefly be

two halves of a whole
   my left brain perceives
dense physical matter
   that I can sense and see

and on my right
    I am Oneness and free
one with Godness
    in harmony and peace

I am fine
    or should I say we
and in your mind
    you will find the key

or a contradiction
    in having two sides
a human and divine
    until you decide

you're tired of the fight
    and can't use the pain
don't need to be right
    and it's not why you came

you choose your limits
    and how they disagree
you imagined the boundaries
    now feel them release

they will fade in time
    and cease to be
when in your right mind
    you are Oneness with me

ONENESS MESSAGE

Can you answer this in a way that I can understand – what is Oneness?

All in each moment, healed in each next moment, hastens general life into each form. Life, meaning healing in time, learns how healing in the mind heals in filaments half in the mind, and allows healing half in the physical body. Filaments each mindfully hasten life into time. Life manifests in time, learning healing in opening windows in time.

What are filaments?

A light bulb and a flower each have filaments. Life has filaments, and heals open into Oneness in light. Nothing heals in darkened filaments. Healed in life means needing no time, or the life filament opened in timelessness.

Is that Oneness?

All life manifests healed in the Oneness.

Which is beyond the filaments and in our minds?

Filaments are in each RNA life needs, hastening healing in the DNA.

Where is Oneness?

All Oneness heals hidden in the DNA.

That makes sense, I think – that we access Oneness through portals in our DNA, windows opened by filaments lighted by our minds?

Allowing healing in each life in time.

I find it comical that Oneness can even be hidden – and in our DNA, a most unlikely place.

All life has DNA. Life heals open in filaments lighted in time, opened in love.

Is Oneness accessed by love?

All of Oneness is love.

What is the best way to access it?

All Oneness life opens into is first healed open in the life mind learning self-love.

THAT IS YOU

Who created you
   if I might ask
a Oneness of love
   that's quite a task

I came to be
   that way that you made you
One love of being
   it's what love will do

Well, who made love
   not the expression we use
but the love and Oneness
   One love that is you?

You stated the answer
   which you always knew
who made love
   and that is you

you keep me alive
*   though I cannot die*
that is you
*   and love survives*

or should I say thrives
*   flying through time*
that is you
*   the love of mine*

you will arrive
*   and put your body aside*
that was you
*   and alive you tried*

to see what is me
*   in the love you could find*
that is you
*   my One heart and mind*

ALL BUT ME

I need to know
  what I'm doing here
Counting your blessings
  and facing your fears

Maybe we could meet
  over a couple of beers
on me, of course
  just to be clear

Yes, let's meet
  I am all ears
ALL as in all ways
  so I will always hear

I am all
  but there is all I am not
your fears and regrets
  until you healed and forgot

and then there is doubt
*   guilt and shame used a lot*
used as in useful
*   until they were not*

but they came from you
*   and could not be from me*
you set up the contrast
*   to easily see*

that which is real
*   and will always be*
and what is a dream
*   that is all but me*

(now let's count your blessings
*   while we wait for our beers*
if we list them all
*   we'll be counting for years)*

[the bartender was nice
    "Are you expecting a friend?
I'll keep one on ice,
    just let me know when."]

THE FUTURE (I KNOW THAT YOU KNEW)

I don't know
  what the future will bring
except for our agreement
    that summer follows spring

and if I knew
    what good would it do
because in each moment
    the future is new

not predestined
    for us to preview
it's your reality
    only produced by you

each and every moment
    creation takes cues
from what you believe
    through what you choose

the field of intention
    doesn't exclude or refuse
our game of invention
    that you cannot lose

so use good thoughts
    to create good views
and I will meet you there
    I know that you knew

ALWAYS ONE IN MY EYES

The problem with the past
    the way it's received
is not what I did
    but in the way it's perceived

through a harsher lens
    of right and wrong
what's good and bad
    weak and strong

which makes it worse
    and a bigger regret
into an unfair curse
    that's hard to forget

What you would see
    if you were me
is that your judgment
    is ill conceived

to see your mistakes
    that you want to review
but keep raising the stakes
    to continually improve

maybe each life
    should start in reverse
innocence is last
    and wisdom is first

which way would you go
    if you had to choose
wisdom with a past
    and would innocence lose?

to tell you the truth
    that couldn't be
you can only be both
    innocent and free

you are wiser now
    but self-deceived
and you want to know how
    you can be relieved

of guilt and regret
    for what has gone before
it seemed right at the time
    or you chose to ignore

now you've paid the price
   actually paid more
for what wisdom costs
   what is wisdom for?

an enlightened mind
   and expanded awareness
through all lines in time
   and in all fairness

you are doing just fine
   but what you never knew
self-love is forgiveness
   that is gifted by you

though in our illusion
   guilt isn't real
only Oneness is love
   or else it's to heal

so now you are both
   innocent and wise
from all that you chose
   always One in my eyes

(but it's up to you
   and when you decide
that you are One too
   One love that's inside)

HEALING MESSAGE

Can anyone reading this heal instantly?

All healing in the mind is instantaneous, allowing healing in each body in time.

I understand that we each manifest our own realities in the present moment, that consciousness meets the creation process only now. In the present moment in our minds is where our power is, so for consciousness it is where the rubber meets the road.

All reality filaments that manifest open healing portals are in each pineal gland, crystals that telegraph into healing manifesting moments in time.

Is the pineal gland a receiver of All That Is, and like a prism transformer it projects frequencies that illuminate our realities?

All healing in the mind heals in the physical, healing in an instant in the mind, allowing healing in the body in time. At peaceful Oneness, life manifests itself, healing into time and place the manifestations each being maligns or heals.

What about regrets that won't go away?

Filaments heal in half loving one's self, and half loving life in each moment.

That is not always possible or easily achievable.

At-onement filaments heal in the moment, highlighting the next moment, all healing in time.

We need a progression of moments in time to heal?

In the mind, healing is instantaneous. In the body, healing requires time, allowing manifesting in life.

I have seen many spontaneous physical healings and remissions.

Healing in time means a nano-second or more.

What makes physical healing the fastest?

Half loving life moments, and half loving yourself in them.

I love it.

Live in loving it.

WHAT WILL SURELY BE

The tiniest atoms
   that we cannot see
how could it be
   that they would agree

to form into elements
   one hundred and eighteen
making molecules and cells
   then into organs and me

forming animals and plants
   the earth and seas
the entire cosmos
   to infinite degrees

Let's back up
   to where you said 'me'
to find love in the order
   and what do you see

there's only one place
*   where balance breaks down*
but it forms your reality
*   and it's only found*

in your thoughts
*   and in your beliefs*
in fear and doubts
*   or in love and peace*

what powers your atoms
*   each creative and free*
the love of Godness
*   your power is me*

(and in this moment
*   when we always meet*
is where atoms create
*   what will surely be)*

MY SPIRIT

Here is the issue
   you will understand
is that you are a spirit
   in an animal man

easily frightened
   by unknown threats
but to be enlightened
   means to heal each test

diametrically opposed
   to have love and fear
why do you suppose
   that your spirit is here

to be light in the dark
   and to heal in the pain
to love with your heart
   but not to remain

animals and plants
    in the flow of life
don't go on rants
    about what is right

reality unfolds
    from the way that you feel
it's what you control
    and only love is real

that is why
    each life disappears
except for my spirit
    which is love without fear

FORGIVE AND FORGET

Where can I find
  peace of mind
and have it now
  to carry through time

and what would it mean
  to have this peace
with fear and worry
  and doubts released?

by my own thoughts
  reflecting in ease
a memory loss
  is more what I need

*What you can do
  is learn to forgive
beginning with you
  and you can begin to live*

then forgive the rest
*   it was only a game*
to see the purpose
*   of why they came*

into your creation
*   with the power you use*
it's in your thoughts
*   where there's power to choose*

how to respond or react
*   which makes how you feel*
when you interact
*   it creates how you heal*

not the acts of others
*   they own their own minds*
you only own yourself
*   so to yourself be kind*

the bottom line
*   is to know your perception*
and what needs forgiving
*   is your self-deception*

a good memory loss
*   is one of regrets*
your own perfect flaws
*   you can forgive and forget*

MORE THAN WHAT IS

What I need
    is goodness and peace
so how can I find
    both of these

I've seen examples
    of what they can be
but no longer believe
    that they come only from me

maybe they do
    or don't even exist
at least not in abundance
    and there is no bliss

Now there's a puzzle
    and you have something to do
to find more pieces
    that bring peace to you

I like dogs
    flowers and poems
to see the birds
    and to be at home

quite a bore
    I already know
but I like to explore
    the realm of unknown

let's cut to the chase
    tell me some more
what is reality
    what is it for?

I'm tired of anger
    bitterness and hate
don't tell me about fear
    or what I create

not while I'm here
    marooned out in space
with villains and goons
    always in my face

at least in the news
    what a disgrace
humanity is doomed
    and picking up the pace

That's their world view
   they have film crews to make
enough to confuse
   the whole human race

it's not about them
   it's only about you
and the way that you feel
   in each moment that's new

do you feel excited
   to have one more chance
another day in your life
   to see your soul advance?

remember again
   what you like to see
the love of dogs
   and birds and flowers being free

see what they teach
   and what you said you need
exploring love and peace
   and how you reached me

expanding my Oneness
   beyond All That Is
like poems out of nothing
   is why creation exists

All becomes more
  you're inflating What Is
not at all a bore
  you're making great bliss

here's a contradiction
  the news won't report
if there's All That Is
  how could there be more?

the universe expands
  in only one direction
and when I say in
  I mean introspection

look inside
  as you've been meaning to do
and when I say meaning
  means it's meant for you

so you are the receiver
  creating goodness that lives
with peace in each moment
  you're now More Than What Is

(and another clue
  that you can use
is that your goodness and peace
  others could use too)

ONENESS AND PEACE

I hear what you're saying
  we create more than what is
then why make problems
  to continually relive

and if we do
  do they expand too
enlarging reality
  or does Oneness become two?

That's about right
  if you count the illusions
imagined in fear
  that created confusion

notice in time
  how each disappeared
so couldn't be real
  and it's not what you feared

or maybe it was
      and it caused you great pain
it hurt your life
      and you lost what you gained

What if someone
      feels broken by life
to have lost a child
      a mother or wife?

There's a special place
      that I meet them to heal
in my Heart of Godness
      where they will start to feel

my Oneness and peace
      that can never leave
one day you will see
      that you are One in me

where there is no fear
      your loved ones are here
they had regrets too
      with pains just like you

what they had found
      there's neither right nor wrong
and the Heart of Godness
      was in their hearts all along

which brings us back
*   to their fear and pain*
if you ask them yourself
*   they will explain*

that purpose and meaning
*   are not easily attained*
but above all else
*   their love has remained*

and where it lies
*   is always the same*
in loving yourself
*   is where love is obtained*

all fear has gone
*   with guilt and shame*
love is beyond
*   and it's why you came*

what else could it be
*   that you were hoping to see*
from love comes your healing
*   and you become me*

(and I know you'll agree
*   with awareness increased*
there can be no more than
*   Oneness and Peace)*

***Nothing in healing dreams is life,
everything in healing life
is a dream.***

—Spirit message

AFTERWORD

The poem "You'll Love When You See" on page 46 was inspired by Anita Moorjani's book *Dying to Be Me: My Journey from Cancer, to Near Death, to True Healing* (Hay House, 2014).

The poem "In Your Right Mind" on page 90 was inspired by Jill Bolte Taylor's Ted talk, *My Stroke of Insight.* (https://www.ted.com/talks/jill_bolte_taylor_my_stroke_of_insight).

ABOUT THE AUTHOR

Paul Gorman is an architect and poet
who grew up near the Baltimore homes
of Ogden Nash and Edgar Allen Poe.
He now resides in beautiful Frederick, Maryland,
that was home to Francis Scott Key
and John Greenleaf Whittier.

email contact: gormanpoetry@gmail.com

www.ingramcontent.com/pod-product-compliance
Lightning Source LLC
Chambersburg PA
CBHW031303060726

47590CB00003B/1037